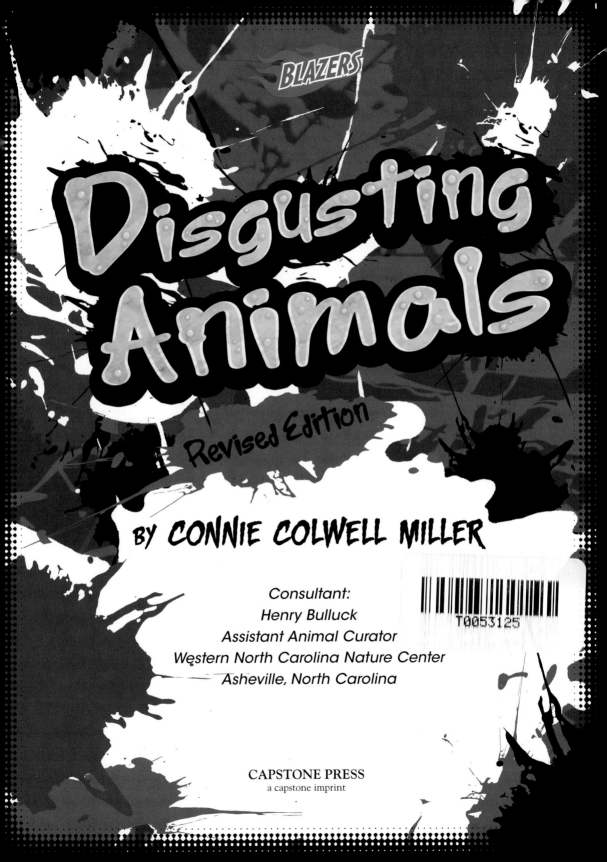

BLAZERS

Disgusting Animals

Revised Edition

BY CONNIE COLWELL MILLER

Consultant:
Henry Bulluck
Assistant Animal Curator
Western North Carolina Nature Center
Asheville, North Carolina

T0053125

CAPSTONE PRESS
a capstone imprint

Blazers is published by Capstone Press,
1710 Roe Crest Drive, North Mankato, Minnesota, 56003
www.mycapstone.com

*Library of Congress Cataloging-in-Publication Data is available on the Library of
Congress Website*

ISBN: 978-1-5157-6275-1 (revised paperback)
ISBN: 978-1-5157-6276-8 (ebook pdf)

Summary: Describes 10 disgusting animals and what makes them gross.

Editorial Credits
Mandy Robbins, editor; Thomas Emery, designer; Bob Lentz, illustrator;
    Jo Miller, photo researcher/photo editor

Photo Credits
AP Photo: Steven Senne, 23 (inset)
Ardea: John Cancalosi, 12-13, Pat Morris, 22-23
Nature Picture Library: Jim Clare, 24-25, Simon Wagen/J. Downer Product, 8-9
Shutterstock: Andrea Izzotti, 11, Anna Moskvina, 14-15, Crystal Kirk, 20-21, Daniel Gale, 4-5,
    Dr. Morley Read, 11 (inset), Geoffrey Kuchera, 16-17, Jakkrit Orrasri, 6-7,
    javarman, cover, Johanna Boomsma, 18-19, Linda George, 28-29, Luca Vaime, 26-27

Printed and bound in the USA.
009969R

Table of Contents

That's Disgusting!

Cats lick their rear ends. Seems pretty gross to humans, but it's how cats keep clean.

Most people enjoy
watching animals.
But don't get too
close! Animals have
some nasty habits.

GROSS-O-METER

Use this meter to gauge how
disgusting these jobs really are.

THAT'S DISGUSTING

Chew on This

After eating, cattle cough up their food and chew it again. The chewed-up food is called cud. Chewing cud helps cattle digest their food.

GROSS-O-METER

SORT OF DISGUSTING

Cattle chew their cud for up to eight hours a day.

Stinky Stuff

Fulmar chicks spray stinky stomach oil to keep enemies away. These birds can shoot the oil almost 7 feet.

GROSS-O-METER

SORT OF DISGUSTING

Bird Barf

Owls swallow mice, birds, and insects whole. After eating, they throw up pellets of fur, bones, teeth, and feathers.

GROSS-O-METER

SORT OF DISGUSTING

Owl pellet

Blood Bath

A frightened horned lizard will shoot blood from its eyes. The blood distracts enemies and gives the lizard a chance to get away.

GROSS-O-METER

SORT OF DISGUSTING

BLAZER FACT

Horned lizards can squirt blood as far as 4 feet.

Green and Gross

Llamas spit at each other to guard their meals. They can spew smelly green goo up to 15 feet.

GROSS-O-METER

PRETTY DISGUSTING

BLAZER FACT

Llama slobber smells so bad, it makes other llamas lose their appetites.

Stink Out

Scaring a skunk can have lasting effects. A frightened skunk will spray a stinky mist out of its behind. The smell can stick around for two years!

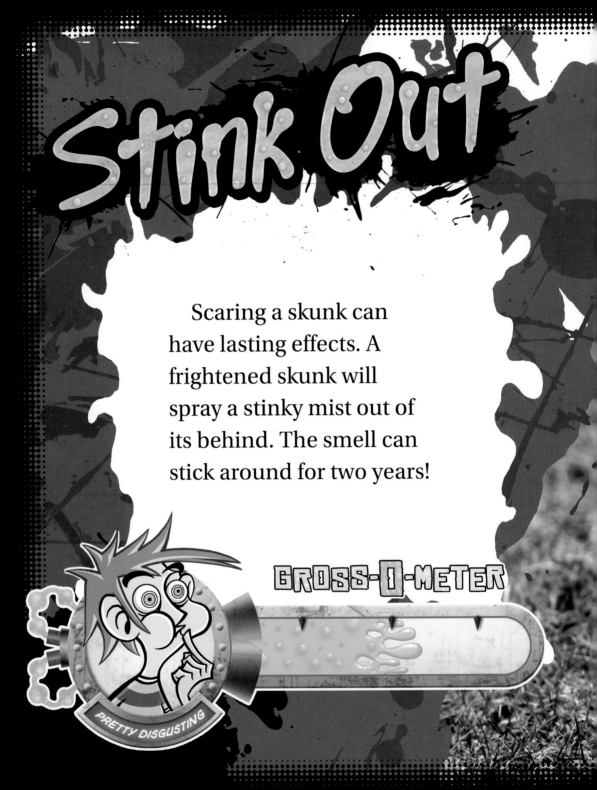

GROSS-O-METER

PRETTY DISGUSTING

Some skunks can spray as far as 23 feet.

Playing Dead

Opossums make enemies think they are already dead. A scared opossum rolls onto its side and sticks out its tongue. Then it poops on itself.

GROSS-O-METER

PRETTY DISGUSTING

Rotting Flesh

Black widow spiders shoot poison into their prey. The poison rots the animal's insides. Then the spider sucks them out.

GROSS-O-METER

PRETTY DISGUSTING

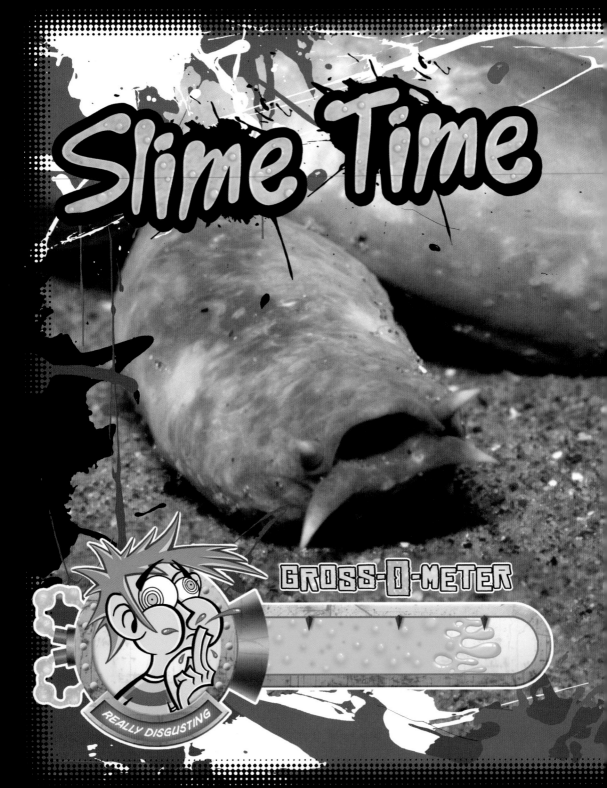

Slime Time

GROSS-O-METER

REALLY DISGUSTING

Hagfish are long, slimy fish with nasty eating habits. A hagfish will squeeze inside a dead animal and eat its way out.

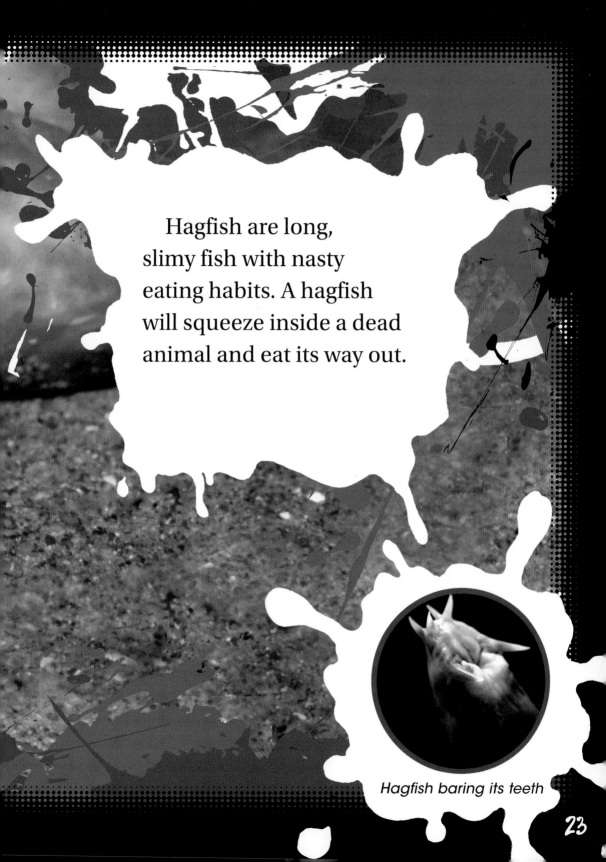

Hagfish baring its teeth

Blood Suckers

Vampire bats drink the blood of cattle, horses, and pigs. Their spit keeps the animal's blood flowing until the bat is full.

GROSS-O-METER

REALLY DISGUSTING

BLAZER FACT

A vampire bat's spit numbs its victim's skin, so the animal can't feel the bite.

The Bite That Kills

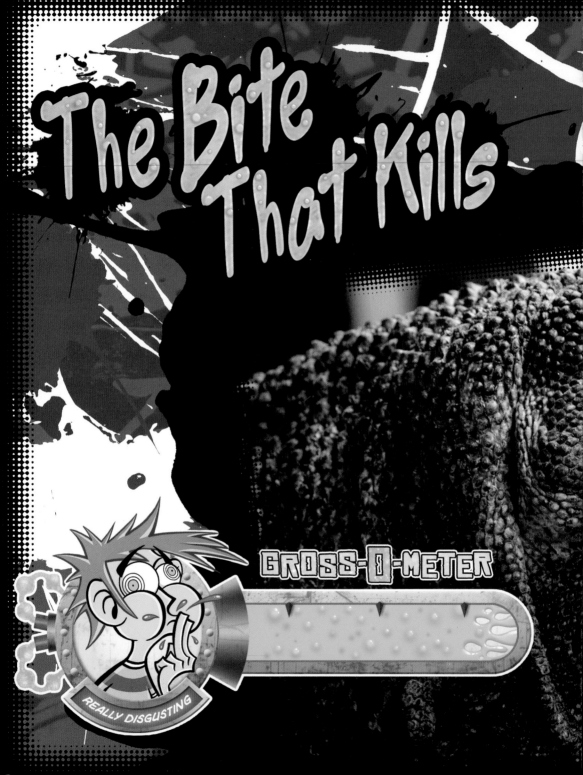

GROSS-O-METER

REALLY DISGUSTING

The komodo dragon's mouth is so dirty, just one bite is deadly. The germs in its saliva can kill almost any animal—even people.

Dirty Behavior

Pigs eat almost anything, including cattle poop. And humans eat pigs!

Animals throw up. They spit. They spray stuff out of their behinds. But all of these disgusting behaviors help animals survive.

We made it through, and I have one thing to say. That's disgusting!

Glossary

cud (KUHD)—food that has not been digested that cows bring up to chew again

digest (dye-JEST)—to break down food so that it can be used by the body

enemy (EN-uh-mee)—an animal that wants to harm or kill another animal

fulmar (FUHL-mahr)—a bird similar to a sea gull that lives in very cold regions of the world

germ (JURM)—a very small living organism that can cause disease

pellet (PEL-it)—a mass of undigested hair, fur, and bones vomited by an owl

prey (PRAY)—an animal that is hunted by another animal for food

saliva (suh-LYE-vuh)—the clear liquid in the mouth

Read More

Murphy, Patricia J. *Why Do Some Animals Shed Their Skin?* The Library of Why. New York: PowerKids Press, 2004.

Branzei, Sylvia. *Animal Grossology: The Science of Creatures Gross and Disgusting.* New York: Penguin Young Readers Group, 2004.

Szpirglas, Jeff. *Gross Universe: Your Guide to All Disgusting Things Under the Sun.* Toronto: Maple Tree Press, 2004.

Internet Sites

FactHound offers a safe, fun way to find Internet sites related to this book. All of the sites on FactHound have been researched by our staff.

Here's how:

1. Visit *www.facthound.com*

2. Choose your grade level.

3. Type in this book ID **073686797X** for age-appropriate sites. You may also browse subjects by clicking on letters, or by clicking on pictures and words.

4. Click on the **Fetch It** button.

FactHound will fetch the best sites for you!

Index